Understand
Your Bible

Understand
Your Bible

John A. Beck

BARBOUR
PUBLISHING

ISBN 978-1-61626-206-8

Published by Barbour Publishing, Inc., P.O. Box 719,
Uhrichsville, Ohio 44683 www.barbourbooks.com

*Our mission is to publish and distribute inspirational products
offering exceptional value and biblical encouragement to the masses.*

 Member of the
Evangelical Christian
Publishers Association

Printed in the United States of America.

In loving memory of my mother,
Lorraine Beck,
who led me to love and to understand
God's Word.

Contents

Introduction

Does your desire to read the Bible often clash with the frustration you feel when you do? The Bible is the bestselling book of all time, which means it's likely there is at least one Bible in almost every home in America. But it's also very likely that those Bibles go unread, in part because the Bible can be difficult to understand. If this describes your situation and you have a desire to dig more deeply into God's Word, then you've come to the right place.

An unread Bible is like an unopened treasure chest.

An unread Bible is like an unopened treasure chest because it contains precious insights that can be acquired from no other source. In the pages of scripture, God tenderly addresses our feelings of guilt and shame. He offers advice on improving our relationships and on raising our children.

He reveals the pathway of wisdom and the secrets of true success. He offers vital words of encouragement when we're down and can't see a way out of our difficult circumstances. And He reveals His deep love for us and His desire to know us intimately— and for us to know Him. Given all that we have to gain, it makes sense that we would want to find the key to this bounty of spiritual treasure.

The Bible Can Be Clear

In many places, the language of the Bible is unmistakably plain, leaving no room for misinterpretation. For example, when the Bible describes the consequences of our sinful rebellion, it is both straightforward and startling: "The wages of sin is death" (Romans 6:23). Fortunately, the solution to

In many places, the language of the Bible is unmistakably plain, leaving no room for misinterpretation.

this crisis is presented in language that is crystal clear and comforting: "For God so loved the world that he gave his one and only Son, that whoever believes in him shall not perish but have eternal life" (John 3:16). The same can be said for this divinely inspired declaration of support found in Psalm 46:1: "God is our refuge and strength, an ever-present help in trouble."

The Bible Can Be Confusing

For every clear passage we find in the Bible, it seems there are dozens that challenge and even confound our understanding. For example, what are we to make of this passage from the Law given in Deuteronomy? "Count off seven weeks from the time you begin to put the sickle to the standing grain. Then celebrate the Festival of Weeks to the LORD your God by giving a freewill offering in proportion to the blessing the LORD your God has given you" (Deuteronomy 16:9–10).

Or what can we glean from the long lists of people or places that fill entire pages of our Bibles? The second half of Joshua is notorious for such lists. "This is the inheritance of the tribe of Judah, according to its clans: The southernmost towns of the tribe of Judah in the Negev toward the boundary of Edom were: Kabzeel, Eder, Jagur, Kinah, Dimonah, Adadah, Kedesh, Hazor, Ithnan. . . ." (Joshua 15:20–23).

Even words from the mouth of Jesus can be confusing: "Salt is good, but if it loses its saltiness, how can it be made salty again? It is fit neither for the soil nor for the manure pile; it is thrown out" (Luke 14:34–35).

The Bible is supposed to help us; but passages like these can leave us confused and frustrated. For many people, this means the Bible goes back on the shelf, where it does no good at all.

The Bible Acknowledges It Can Be Confusing
It is striking, and somewhat comforting to know, that the Bible acknowledges

how difficult it can be to understand. The author of Acts introduces us to a confused Bible reader, a well-educated man from the royal court of Ethiopia who had come to Jerusalem to worship in the days following the death and resurrection of Jesus. There is no doubt that, during his visit, he would have heard the news of a man named Jesus who identified Himself as the promised Savior of the world and who had miraculously risen from the dead three days after His crucifixion.

As the royal official's chariot bounced from rut to rut on the way home, the man was quietly reading his Bible, trying to make sense of it all. The Holy Spirit directed Philip, a close follower of Jesus, to walk down the same road and approach the chariot. The puzzled look on the Ethiopian's face betrayed the confusion raging in his mind. This prompted Philip to ask a probing question: "Do you understand what you are reading?" "How can I," the

The Bible acknowledges how difficult it can be to understand.

man replied, "unless someone explains it to me?" (Acts 8:30–31).

There you have it. The Bible acknowledges the problem. If a motivated, intelligent reader who lived during the first century—at the very time that some of the events of the Bible were unfolding—can meet obstacles in his Bible reading, we should not feel ashamed when we struggle to understand a portion of God's Word.

We should not feel ashamed when we struggle to understand a portion of God's Word.

This Book Addresses Bible-Reading Confusion

This book has the same goal that Philip had on that desert road: to address the confusion that can accompany Bible reading. At the risk of oversimplification, we can group common misunderstandings of the Bible into six categories, which we will then address in the following six chapters.

In chapter 1 we will answer the question, *What is the Bible?* Our focus will be on both the human and divine sides of its origins. We will consider how the unique beginnings of this book call for us to read the Bible in a way that we read no other book. At times our frustration in reading a Bible passage can be the result of our failure to consider the small details in the larger context of the big ideas that God wants to share with us.

Some of our confusion in reading the Bible can be attributed to reading one type of writing with rules meant to apply to another.

The second chapter introduces five big ideas that God shares again and again in the Bible. We will see how reading passages that confuse us in light of these big ideas can improve our understanding and help us to answer the question, *What is God talking about?*

The third chapter raises the question, *How is God speaking?* Although the Bible is bound as a single volume and conveys the message of a single author—that is, God

Himself—the style of writing varies from book to book and can even change within a book. Some of our confusion in reading the Bible can be attributed to reading one type of writing with rules meant to apply to another. Chapter 3 introduces the primary categories of literature (genres) we find in the Bible and offers general suggestions on how to read each most profitably.

The fourth chapter is governed by the question, *What is going on behind the scenes?* In almost all cases, the depth of our understanding will grow when we develop a better understanding of historical context. This is certainly true when we read the New Testament epistles—ancient letters delivered to specific people living in a specific place at a specific time and dealing with specific issues. But it is also true of Bible stories in general that a broader understanding of the historical context will shed light on the words and actions found in the narrative.

Cultural context can be as important to our understanding of the Bible as historical context. That's why in chapter 5 we'll tackle the question, *What are they doing?* Because the Bible describes the lives of people who lived in a distant land and far removed from our modern age, we can expect to find references to food, dress, manners, and customs that are very different from our own. The description of such practices and devices, as well as their use in figures of speech, may challenge our understanding until we deepen our awareness of the Bible's cultural context.

Cultural context can be as important to our understanding of the Bible as historical context.

Finally, we'll come to the question, *Where am I?* Many Bible passages include place names and descriptions of topography, geology, water, flora, fauna, and the ways that people responded to the physical setting in which they lived. Chapter 6 illustrates the value of deepening our awareness of geographical context.

"Do you understand what you are reading?"

You may not be reading your Bible while bouncing along in a chariot after a visit to Jerusalem. But like the Ethiopian official, you may be challenged and frustrated by not being able to fully comprehend what God is saying in the Bible. My prayer is that the following discussion will give new direction to your Bible reading and will lead to rewarding insights and a greater passion to read your Bible on a regular basis. Read on—exciting discoveries lie just ahead!

What Is the Bible?

When we meet someone for the first time, our early exchanges are often governed by carefully choreographed questions through which we learn more about one another. *Where do you live? Where did you go to school? What do you do for a living?* The answers to these and other questions about family, interests, and hobbies provide the foundation for friendship and further interaction.

The information we gather when meeting someone new is similar to the information gathering we do when we pick up a book for the first time. We turn it over in our hands and examine the cover, the table of contents, and the author's biography to get some idea of what the book is all about and whether a sustained "conversation" with the author might be worth our time.

Our approach to the Bible is no different. To understand what the Bible says, we would do well first to ask, "What is it?" The Bible looks very much like any other book—whether it's one we've pulled from the shelf, downloaded onto a portable reading device, or opened on a computer screen. Yet the truth of the matter is that the Bible is different from the children's books in our kids' rooms; different from our college textbooks, our technical manuals, and our novels; and different from the cookbooks in the kitchen.

In this chapter we will see that the Bible is a very unique book, because it has both a divine and a human side to its origins. We'll take a look at the Bible's unique origins, see the important implications of those origins, and illustrate how knowing what the Bible *is* will change the way we read and engage with its contents.

> *The Bible is a very unique book, because it has both a divine and a human side to its origins.*

The Human Side

Experience teaches that a well-crafted page of writing, with appropriately formed sentences and paragraphs, is not produced by plants or random animals. Neither is it the product of a strong wind blowing arbitrary words off the page of a dictionary. So when we look at the pages of the Bible, we can safely assume that a human author has been at work. The truth of the matter is that the Bible has many human authors, representing a wide range of times, places, occupations, and circumstances.

Moses is widely regarded as the author of the first five books of the Bible. He started writing in about 1450 BC. On a timeline, that's more than 2,800 years before the invention of the printing press, nearly 3,200 years before the signing of the U.S. Constitution, and more than 3,400 years before today. At the other end of the spectrum, the most recent books of the Bible date to the first century AD—closer to our modern day, but still nearly 2,000 years removed. To

The sixty-six books of the Bible were composed by a variety of human authors between the fifteenth century BC and the first century AD.

sum it all up, the sixty-six books of the Bible were composed by a variety of human authors between the fifteenth century BC and the first century AD—a span of more than 1,500 years.

When they wrote they put pen to paper in many different locations, from Africa to the Middle East, and from Europe to Asia. As we might expect, some of the books were written within the borders of the Promised Land, Israel. Other writers of the Bible wrote in places as distant and distinct as Egypt, Babylon (modern-day Iraq), Asia Minor (modern-day Turkey), and Corinth (which is in Greece).

The writers of the Bible also came from a variety of backgrounds. Some were leaders, such as Moses and Samuel; or prophets, such as Isaiah, Jeremiah, Ezekiel, and Obadiah. But also among the recognized writers we find kings, such as David and Solomon; a physician (Luke); a Roman tax collector (Matthew); fishermen, such as Peter and John; and Amos, who identifies himself as both a shepherd and a fig farmer (see Amos 7:14).

Coming, as they did, from across the timeline and geographical boundaries of the ancient world, the authors of the books of the Bible composed their poetry and prose from a wide range of personal circumstances. They knew both good times and bad. Some had celebrated the birth of children; others had experienced the heady rewards of business or political success. We also meet authors whose lives were beset by personal tragedy—the loss of a child, a wayward wife, or exile in a foreign country. We meet some who are struggling spiritually in the wake of serious sins like murder or adultery. Still others had to deal with rebellious children, personal depression, military invasion, or time spent in prison. As real people living in real places in real time, the authors of the Bible saw life in all its glory and all its disappointments.

As real people living in real places in real time, the authors of the Bible saw life in all its glory and all its disappointments.

The Implications of Human Authorship

Because the human authors of the Bible experienced life in all its fullness, we feel the humanness in what they've written. We resonate with their joys and feel the wrenching of their sorrows. We hear their laughter and see the tears that stained the pages on which they wrote. We rejoice in their victories and feel the disappointment of the losses that threatened to rob them of hope. In all these experiences and feelings—which are very real to us—we can quickly and easily immerse ourselves in the pages of this great book.

The Divine Side

What makes the Bible so unique is that it also has a divine side to its origins. The eternal God, who is both creator and ultimate ruler of our world, clearly has a passion to speak to us. Though He has spoken individually and directly to people in the past—or at least as directly as we mortals can endure—in most cases, God has chosen to communicate in writing, using a very unique process of composition that involves both a human and a divine author working in concert.

Within the Bible we find reference to this unique phenomenon, which has been called *divine inspiration*. Just as God animated the lifeless flesh of the first human being by breathing into his nostrils "the breath of life" (Genesis 2:7), so we are told that "all Scripture is God-breathed" (2 Timothy 3:16). The human authors of the Bible who received this "breath of God" tapped into a knowledge base bigger than their own. The apostle Paul puts it this way in 1 Corinthians 2:13: "This is what we speak, not in words taught us by human wisdom but in words taught by the Spirit, explaining spiritual realities with Spirit-taught words." At times we get the impression that these human authors were

God has chosen to communicate in writing, using a very unique process of composition.

barely keeping up during this process. Peter says, "Prophets, though human, spoke from God as they were carried along by the Holy Spirit" (2 Peter 1:21).

The phrase *divine inspiration* captures the essence and mystery of the process. The English word *inspiration* comes from the Latin *inspirare*, which means "to breathe in." In this case inspiration is not merely a brilliant flash of insight. It is more than the ability to scan the horizon of the human experience and capture the essentials with just the right words. The writing process that resulted in the Bible was both informed and directed by the Holy Spirit. In the end God communicated precisely what He intended to say, yet in ways that reflected the unique experiences, knowledge, perceptions, and writing styles of the human authors. God spoke through these writers, yet without abolishing the uniqueness of their human contribution.

The writing process that resulted in the Bible was both informed and directed by the Holy Spirit.

The Implications of Divine Authorship

If you're a bit confused by this description of the biblical writing process, that's not surprising. No one fully understands how God accomplished His purpose in giving us the Bible, but we can quickly see the implications and the importance of divine authorship. First of all, it means that what we read in the Bible is true. Left to their own devices, the human authors of the Bible were entirely capable of selecting the wrong word or of making a mistake in reporting the details of an event. God, on the other hand, is incapable of error. As the Holy Spirit directed the writing process, He made sure that these authors rose above the horizon of their mortal limitations so that what they wrote came to us in untarnished form.

If you're a bit confused by this description of the biblical writing process, that's not surprising.

When Jesus prayed for His disciples, He called attention to this striking quality of divine speech: "Sanctify them by the truth; your word is truth" (John 17:17). Though the Bible was written thousands of years ago, in a time before computers, cameras, and video recorders, we can be assured that these writers knew what they were talking about because their writing was overseen by God Himself. God's Word is true.

The Bible's truthfulness and reliability make it a "must read" book. Other books may rise quickly on the *New York Times* bestseller list and clamor for our attention. Such well-crafted books have the power to entertain, inform, and guide us.

Only in the Bible do we hear God speaking to us directly and candidly.

But every one of those books fails to rise above human limitations. Only in the Bible do we hear God speaking to us directly and candidly. Of all the books that have ever been published—or that ever will be published—the Bible is the only one we *must* read and understand.

Illustration

Because the Bible has such a unique heritage, we read it differently than we do other books. When we read an ordinary book, we evaluate its integrity based on our knowledge of the author and his or her credentials—particularly when the author is challenging us to think or act in a certain way. For example, if I'm reading a book about raising my kids, I'm going to reserve judgment on the book's usefulness and value until I've evaluated the

The unique origins of the Bible change the way we read and respond to its message and application.

author's knowledge, expertise, and approach. If the author makes suggestions that fall outside the realm of what seems practical or credible, that book is likely to find itself on the resale shelf. The unique origins of the Bible, on the other hand, change the way we read and respond to its message and application. Because of its divine authorship, presented through the lives and words of human writers, the Bible can challenge us to believe the unbelievable and do the unthinkable.

Heavenly Math

God makes every effort to reveal His true identity within the pages of the Bible. Yet we can have difficulty understanding what He is telling us. In some places the Bible clearly declares that God is one: "Hear, O Israel: The LORD our God, the LORD is one" (Deuteronomy 6:4). In other places God speaks of Himself in the plural (see Genesis 1:26), and Jesus calls for the recognition of God as three distinct persons: "Therefore go and make disciples of all nations, baptizing them in the name of the Father and of the Son and of the Holy Spirit" (Matthew 28:19).

So is God three or is God one? Our earthbound math limits us to one of those two options. But the God who created our world—and mathematics—lives beyond such limitations. That's why He can describe Himself as both three and one at the same time: 1 + 1 + 1 = 1. If I were reading any other book, I might quickly dismiss that idea as preposterous. Yet, because I know that "the foolishness of God is wiser than human wisdom" (1 Corinthians 1:25), I read the Bible in a different way. When I recognize the Bible as God's own book, I can ponder these equations and nod my head in agreement, marveling at a mystery that exceeds my comprehension.

Radical Love

The Bible not only calls for us to believe the unbelievable, but it also can call us to do the unthinkable. Each day, we make decisions—both consciously and unconsciously—about how we will treat the people around us. As we interact with other drivers on the roadway, with salesclerks at the store, and with our family members,

The Bible not only calls for us to believe the unbelievable, but it also can call us to do the unthinkable.

we naturally fall into patterns of extending varying degrees of kindness and courtesy to those who cross our path. If we are honest with ourselves, we tend to reserve the best treatment for those who have proven themselves worthy. In the Bible Jesus calls for us to rethink our habits of interaction. "You have heard that it was said, 'Love your neighbor and hate your enemy.' But I tell you, love your enemies and pray for those who persecute you, that you may be children of your Father in heaven. He causes his sun to rise on the evil and the good, and sends rain on the righteous and the unrighteous" (Matthew 5:43–45). Common sense might suggest that this is an unthinkable course of action. Should we not reward those who treat us well with the best treatment and withhold kindness from those who mean us harm? But here the Bible encourages us to take God's perspective—to lavish sunshine and rain on those who treat Him well and those who do

The Bible encourages us to take God's perspective.

not. As the Bible calls for us to believe the unbelievable, it also calls for us to do what at first blush seems unthinkable.

Bible References

As a book the Bible is somewhat unique in that it has a tiered set of divisions, which allows quick reference to even its shortest parts.

First, the Bible is divided into two testaments. Generally speaking, the Old Testament is the collection of writings that introduce us to God and to His plan to rescue the world from sin. The New Testament speaks about the realization of the promises made in the Old Testament, focusing largely on the life of Jesus and the history of the church that took shape around His teachings.

The Old Testament is the collection of writings that introduce us to God.

Each of the two testaments is divided into books—thirty-nine in the Old Testament and twenty-seven in the New Testament, for a total of sixty-six. When a Bible reference is given, the first element in the reference is to one of these books.

Each book in the Bible is further divided into chapters, and each chapter is subdivided into verses. If someone wishes to call attention to a specific sentence or paragraph in the Bible, he or she will typically not use a page number (which varies from one version of the Bible to the next), but will point to the reference by identifying the book, chapter, and verse(s). It will look like this: Matthew 5:1–12. In this case, the reference is to the New Testament book of Matthew, chapter 5, verses 1 through 12.

English Versions

The human authors of the Bible expressed themselves in three languages—Hebrew, Aramaic, and Greek—all of which are unfamiliar to most modern readers. That means our English versions are translations from those languages.

If you read the same Bible passage in more than one English version, you will likely find some differences. English translations differ from one another in two ways. First, the Bible translators worked with principles that guided their translation efforts for a particular version. Sometimes the goal is to remain as close as possible to the language structure of the parent text, even if that makes the translation sound somewhat less natural to native English speakers. Alternatively, the translator may have sought to produce a translation that sounds very natural in English, even if it diverges from the original images and language structure of the parent text.

The human authors of the Bible expressed themselves in three languages—Hebrew, Aramaic, and Greek.

Bible translations also vary from one another in that they are targeting the vocabulary and style of a particular group of

English speakers. Vocabulary and grammar change with time and location and within subgroups that live within a certain time and place. For that reason the translators must choose a particular form of English to use, to make their translation readable by their intended audience. So, for example, the King James Version of the Bible was written in the style of English used in Great Britain in the seventeenth century, and the New Living Translation is written in more contemporary, modern English.

Each type of translation has its place. If you would like to learn more about the translation philosophy that guided your English translation, read the preface of your Bible. This is where the Bible's publisher typically discusses the translation philosophy that guided their version of the Bible.

What Is God Talking About?

Bible reading can become very frustrating when we get bogged down in sentences, paragraphs, or even pages filled with apparently meaningless details. When we encounter portions of God's Word like this, we may well ask, "What is God talking about?" In many respects, it is like joining a conversation that is already in progress. At first all we may hear in the conversation are references to people, places, and actions that seem unrelated to one another. Only after we have listened for a while and understand the bigger ideas being discussed can we make sense of the smaller details. The same is true of our Bible reading. It is most helpful to know the big ideas that God shares

It is most helpful to know the big ideas that God shares with us in the Bible so that the smaller details can find their place among them.

with us in the Bible so that the smaller details can find their place among them.

The Obstacle

Some sections of the Bible come at us like an avalanche. The images and ideas tumble over one another and threaten to sweep us off the mountain, turning us head over heels before burying us in the suffocating darkness of too much detail. That verbal avalanche often strikes us when we read a chapter that contains a long list of laws, some of which sound particularly strange to the modern ear:

"Do not cook a young goat in its mother's milk" (Exodus 34:26).

"Keep my decrees. Do not mate different kinds of animals" (Leviticus 19:19).

"Do not eat any meat with the blood still in it" (Leviticus 19:26).

"Do not plow with an ox and a donkey yoked together. Do not wear clothes of wool and linen woven together" (Deuteronomy 22:10–11).

In other sections of the Bible, we encounter long lists of unfamiliar place names to which we have no apparent connection. For example, "The allotment for the trip of Judah, according to its clans, extended down to the territory of Edom, to the Desert of Zin in the extreme south. Their southern boundary started from the bay the at the southern end of the Dead Sea, crossed south of Scorpion Pass, continued on to Zin and went over to the south of Kadesh Barnea" (Joshua 15:1–3).

In still other passages, we encounter lists of people's names, such as in the first chapter of Matthew: "This is the genealogy of Jesus the Messiah the son of David, the son of Abraham: Abraham was the father of Isaac, Isaac the father of Jacob, Jacob the father of Judah and his brothers, Judah the father of Perez and Zerah, whose mother was Tamar, Perez the father of Hezron, Hezron the father of Ram. . ." (Matthew 1:1–3). We rightly presume that God has something to say to us here, but what is it?

The Solution

We can understand the role of Bible passages like these when we become familiar with the five big ideas that God shares with us in His Word. Though the Bible generally moves forward in time from the book of Genesis through the book of Revelation, it also circles back to repeat and emphasize the big ideas that God longs to share with us in our conversation with Him. We will better understand everything in the Bible when we read it with an awareness of those big ideas. Let's consider each in turn.

We will better understand everything in the Bible when we read it with an awareness of those big ideas.

1. There Is Only One God

The authors of the Bible, whether they lived during the time of the Old Testament or the New Testament, lived amid cultures that believed in many gods—multiple deities who competed with one another, often at the expense of us mere mortals.

In complete contrast the Bible affirms that there is just one God. In the very first verse of the Bible, Genesis 1:1, this one God is identified as the creator of all things. There is absolutely no mention of other deities on the eternal stage, either competing with God or supporting His efforts. In the Law of Moses, the very first commandment turns this idea into a divine directive: "You shall have no other gods before me. You shall not make for yourself an image in the form of anything in heaven above or on the earth beneath or in the waters below. You shall not bow down to them or worship them" (Exodus 20:3–5).

This big idea, which is introduced so aggressively in the first two books of the Bible, is repeated again and again in the books that follow. At times this idea is presented directly:

"Hear, O Israel: The LORD our God, the LORD is one" (Deuteronomy 6:4).

"This is what the LORD says—Israel's King and Redeemer, the LORD Almighty: I am the first and I am the last; apart from me there is no God" (Isaiah 44:6).

At other times it is presented as a warning to avoid building and worshipping images that represent the fraudulent deities of the surrounding culture:

"All who make idols are nothing, and the things they treasure are worthless. Those who would speak up for them are blind; they are ignorant, to their own shame" (Isaiah 44:9).

The first big idea is clear: There is only one God.

"Do I mean then that food sacrificed to an idol is anything, or that an idol is anything? No, but the sacrifices of pagans are offered to demons, not to God, and I do not want you to be participants with demons" (1 Corinthians 10:19–20).

The first big idea is clear: There is only one God.

2. God Is Holy, and He Demands That We Be Holy

To be holy is to be unique or set apart from the ordinary. This is a fundamental quality of God's, which He imparted to mortals on the day of their creation (Genesis 1:27). This does not mean that Adam and Eve were gods, but it does mean they were created so that their native passions, desires, and actions were in harmony with God's. So long as Adam and Eve remained holy, as God is holy, they could enjoy His company. However, when they experimented with thinking and actions contrary to God's will, they plunged themselves and their descendants into an unholy state, at enmity with God. As this ruined condition spread down through the generations, it had its impact on the environment and on the human condition.

Even though this change in state occurred for humanity, the prime directive from God had not changed.

Physical pain, strained relationships, weeds in the garden, and the death of those we love are reminders that things changed for the worse after the Fall (see Genesis 3:14–19).

Even though this change in state occurred for humanity, the prime directive from God had not changed: "Be holy because I, the LORD your God, am holy" (Leviticus 19:2). God is not suggesting that we just do the best we can under the circumstances. No, His standard is still perfection. The legal directives that fill the Bible are a reminder of all that God requires. But we all find ourselves in the same situation that the apostle Paul found himself: "For I do not do the good I want to do, but the evil I do not want to do—this I keep on doing" (Romans 7:19). This second big idea—that God is holy and demands that every mortal be holy as well—creates a real dilemma for us.

God is not suggesting that we just do the best we can under the circumstances.

3. God Has a Plan to Restore Us to Holiness

This idea is perhaps the biggest of the big ideas presented in the Bible, because it so radically changes the future of all who will accept it. God's solution to our sin resides in the core principle of *substitution*. As a just God who put the earlier foundation principle in place, God was obligated to punish the rebellion that mortal humans introduced into the world. But He also had a solution to the problem: He could provide a substitute to stand in the place of those who owed God a perfect life but could no longer deliver on their obligation. Furthermore, this substitute, though undeserving of any punishment Himself, would be punished on our behalf, so that the divine obligation to punish sin would no longer be hanging over our heads. In the Old Testament, Isaiah anticipates the coming

God was obligated to punish the rebellion that mortal humans introduced into the world.

of this substitute, Jesus, with vivid language: "Surely he took up our pain and bore our suffering, yet we considered him punished by God, stricken by him, and afflicted. But he was pierced for our transgressions, he was crushed for our iniquities; the punishment that brought us peace was on him, and by his wounds we are healed. We all, like sheep, have gone astray, each of us has turned to our own way; and the LORD has laid on him the iniquity of us all" (Isaiah 53:4–6).

In 2 Corinthians 5:21 the apostle Paul looks back on the life of Jesus and expresses the big idea of substitution in this way: "God made him who had no sin to be sin for us, so that in him we might become the righteousness of God." And what does God ask in payment to receive the benefits of this plan? He asks only that we believe what He has said about us. We are again holy in God's eyes because Jesus did what

We are again holy in God's eyes because Jesus did what we could not do and undid what we had done.

we could not do and undid what we had done.

God's plan to provide a substitute is mentioned immediately after Adam and Eve exchanged their holy state for a sinful state (see Genesis 3:15). As we turn through the pages of the Old Testament, we see the promised plan for substitution described with increasing detail. For example, the

Lord appears to Abram and tells him that, although he is childless at the moment, his offspring will grow to become a great nation. God further promises Abram that his family-turned-nation will occupy a special piece of real estate, the Promised Land of Canaan. Finally, Abram is told that the Savior from sin, the substitute for all mortals, will be a descendant of that nation and be born in the Promised Land (see Genesis 12:1–3). Throughout the Old Testament, the ideas of "nation" and "land" are intimately linked to the big idea of salvation by substitution.

Abram is told that the Savior. . . will be a descendant of that nation.

The promise is further narrowed and focused after the nation of Israel has been formed and King David is ruling as its king. He is told that the coming Savior (Messiah) will be one of his descendants. So, from this time on, the biblical authors also use royal imagery when speaking about the coming of this special substitute. He would be the King who rules an eternal kingdom (see 2 Samuel 7:11–16). The world was holding its breath, waiting for the arrival of this special substitute, when the angel Gabriel appeared to a young girl in the small agricultural village of Nazareth. He had special news for Mary: "You will conceive and give birth to a son, and you are to call him Jesus. He will be great and will be called the Son of the Most High. The Lord God will give him the throne of his father David, and he will reign over Jacob's descendants forever; his kingdom will never end" (Luke 1:31–33).

Jesus did exactly what we needed Him to do for us.

Jesus did exactly what we needed Him to do for us. He intervened to live the life we owed God but could not deliver; He is the one who absorbed the punishment of God headed our way. Paul sums up this big idea in one powerful sentence: "For just as through the disobedience of the one man the many were made sinners, so also through the obedience of the one man the many will be made righteous" (Romans 5:19). This remains the biggest of the big ideas in the Bible.

4. God Wants Us to Enjoy Successful Lives on Earth

Life goes on, and it can be full of challenges—in no small part because those who oppose the coming of God and His kingdom will do all they can to make life more difficult for God's people. How can we find greater success and happiness in the daily lives we lead? The human author of Ecclesiastes tried to find satisfaction and success on earth without turning to the direction that God offered. The result of that experiment in living is captured with words like these:

How can we find greater success and happiness in the daily lives we lead?

"I have seen all the things that are done under the sun; all of them are meaningless, a chasing after the wind" (Ecclesiastes 1:14).

"I denied myself nothing my eyes

desired; I refused my heart no pleasure. My heart took delight in all my labor, and this was the reward for all my toil. Yet when I surveyed all that my hands had done and what I had toiled to achieve, everything was meaningless, a chasing after the wind; nothing was gained under the sun" (Ecclesiastes 2:10–11).

Life in a sin-ruined world can feel like chasing after the wind, even for those who know Jesus as their Savior. But God has no desire for us to live in that frustration. He wants us to find some measure of happiness and success, and so He offers direction for living in the world He created. Some of that direction comes to us in the form of commandments, such as the one that safeguards our personal property: "You shall not steal" (Exodus 20:15). At other times the lesson for living comes to us in story form. A vignette from the story of Joseph illustrates how one can

> *Life in a sin-ruined world can feel like chasing after the wind, even for those who know Jesus as their Savior.*

successfully manage sexual temptation (see Genesis 39). The Proverbs are short axioms that offer general direction on successful living:

"The soothing tongue is a tree of life, but a perverse tongue crushes the spirit" (Proverbs 15:4).

"A hot-tempered person stirs up conflict, but the one who is patient calms the quarrel" (Proverbs 15:18).

Jesus encouraged a perspective change on life, which was designed to mitigate worry (see Matthew 6:25–34). God longs to show us how we can find greater success and happiness in a world that offers precious little of both—which leads us to the fifth and final big idea.

> *The Proverbs are short axioms that offer general direction on successful living.*

5. God Has a Plan for Our Eternal Happiness

In the end the fullest realization of the happiness we seek will always run up against the cold reality that we are looking for perfection in an imperfect world. The fifth big idea presented in the Bible addresses the life that will follow the one we know on earth. Jesus demonstrated His power over death by rising from the tomb on the third day. Part of His plan for our eternal happiness involves the resurrection of our bodies, as well. In speaking with a grieving sister, Jesus laid that reality bare: "I am the resurrection and the life. The one who believes in me will live, even though they die; and whoever lives by believing in me will never die" (John 11:25–26).

The new bodies we will enjoy after death will have a new home that is completely redeemed from the ruin of sin.

The new bodies we will enjoy after death will have a new home that is completely redeemed from the ruin of sin. The apostle John received a brief glimpse into this world. He found language inadequate to express all that he saw, but he shared what he could. In a revelation from God, John saw thousands of people in white robes and inquired about who they were. Here is the answer he received:

"These are they who have come out of the great tribulation; they have washed their robes and made them white in the blood of the Lamb. Therefore, they are before the throne of God and serve him day and night in his temple, and he who sits on the throne will shelter them with his presence. 'Never again will they hunger; never again will they thirst. The sun will not beat down on them,' nor any scorching heat. For the Lamb at the center of the throne will be their shepherd; 'he will lead them to springs of living water.' 'And God will wipe away every tear from their eyes' " (Revelation 7:14–17).

The final book of the Bible returns us to the same themes we found in the first chapter of the Bible. Humans will once again live in perfect harmony with their creator. God has a plan for our eternal happiness.

Illustration

When we encounter a set of verses that don't make much sense on their own, it can be most helpful to see their relationship to one or more of the five big ideas that God repeatedly communicates in His Word. Take, for example, the laws we mentioned earlier. Most of the laws found in the Old Testament were in effect only between the time when God issued them on Mount Sinai and when the Savior completed His work on earth. As promised, the family of Abraham grew to become a great nation. Each member of that nation became a caretaker of the most precious promise God had given the world, the promise to send a Savior. To remind Israel of their special assignment and to distinguish them from all the other nations of the world, God imposed a unique lifestyle

Most of the laws found in the Old Testament were in effect only between the time when God issued them on Mount Sinai and when the Savior completed His work on earth.

on them. He called for them to be holy—that is, to live lives distinguishable from all the other nations of the world. They were to avoid eating meat with the blood still in it, refrain from plowing with an ox and a donkey yoked together, and not wear garments that combined wool and linen. These unique requirements reminded the nation that they were a unique people who served a unique God. These temporary laws that fill the early books of the Bible help us understand how God identified and maintained Israel as a unique people, a nest in which the promise of salvation was incubated.

The long lists of place names we find in the book of Joshua have a similar role to play. At the time of Abraham, the Lord tied the promise of the Savior to the Promised Land. As the one true God who created the world, the Lord had the right to assign property as He saw fit. It was the Lord's desire to make the promise of the coming Savior personal by giving each family a small segment of the Promised Land on which to build their home, grow their grain, and graze their animals. Property does not function for us in that way today; but in the Bible, owning a piece of the Promised Land was how a family could connect itself to God's plan to save the world.

Likewise, the long list of names that opens the book of Matthew plays a very important role in God's plan, as Matthew seeks to link the promises made in the Old Testament with their fulfillment in Jesus Christ. Given all that God had said about the coming Messiah, it became clear that the Savior could not be born into just any family. People such as Abraham, Jacob, Judah, and David had been promised that this special substitute would be a member of their family. In that light Matthew's list makes much more sense. The genealogy begins with Abraham and mentions all the key figures to whom the promise had been made. Joseph, Jesus' earthly father, is mentioned just before Jesus because, among the ancient Israelites, one's genealogical

The long list of names that opens the book of Matthew plays a very important role in God's plan.

heritage was always traced through the father. So this list, which at first blush fails to engage us as readers, actually becomes an important key in identifying Jesus as the substitute sent by God to provide a pathway that restores our relationship with God.

Bible reading can become frustrating when we get bogged down by paragraphs filled with apparently meaningless details. But we can gain a better understanding of these challenging passages when we view them in light of the five big ideas that God desires to communicate in His conversation with us.

How Is God Speaking?

Our eyes touch a wide variety of reading materials in any given week, including business e-mails, advertisements, Tweets, software agreements, novels, and notes sent home from school. Nimbly and without giving it a thought, we change our reading speed, level of attention, and general engagement in order to properly adjust to the text before us. We need to make similar adjustments when we read the Bible. Although one page of the Bible can look very similar to the next, those pages often contain different categories of written communication or genre, which call for us to adjust the way we read them. To best understand what God says to us in His Word, we need to ask how He is speaking to us on a particular page and adjust our reading strategy to match.

The Obstacle

Because we are less familiar with the genres used by the biblical authors and less practiced at the art of reading them, we are less likely to make the necessary shifts in our reading and interpretation style as we move through the Bible. *Genre* is simply a fancy word for a category of writing using a similar style and form. We can think of genre as an unwritten agreement between the author and the reader. Each genre has its own set of reading rules that govern the relationship between reader and text. So, for example, we would read and understand a children's fairy tale in a different way than an online newsmagazine. If we fail to observe the rules of genre, we may leave the book of fairy tales believing that pigs can talk, that wolves dress in Grandma's clothing, and that one needs to be careful about climbing beanstalks grown from magic beans. Of course this sounds

> Genre *is simply a fancy word for a category of writing using a similar style and form.*

ridiculous, but we can make similar errors in our Bible reading when we try to read every page and every book in exactly the same way.

In the Bible, which encompasses several diverse genres, the shifts between genres can occur quickly and with little or no warning. Consider, for example, Judges 4–5. In these two chapters, the Bible describes the same event, the oppression of the Israelites by a Canaanite king and the divinely sponsored victory that released the Israelites from that oppression. In Judges 4 the author uses the genre of historical narrative to report on the event. In Judges 5 the same event is recast as an extended piece of poetry, which is a different genre with different rules. The use of two distinct literary forms to describe the same event serves to emphasize two different dimensions of the story. If we try to read both chapters with the same reading

In the Bible, the shifts between genres can occur quickly and with little or no warning.

strategy, we are likely to miss what God is trying to tell us. That is why we need to ask, "How is God speaking?"

The Solution

We will read the Bible with greater understanding and greater satisfaction when we become familiar with the basic categories of literature, or genres, used, become familiar with the way the books are composed, and acquire basic strategies for reading and interpreting God's message to us. Here we will briefly introduce and illustrate the six types of communication we encounter most frequently in the Bible: historical narrative, poetry, law, prophecy, letters (epistles), and apocalyptic.

Historical Narrative

Historical narrative is the most commonly used genre in the Bible and is found in much of the Old Testament, in the Gospels, and in Acts. In this style of communication, the author takes historical events and turns them into a story. Because events are always composed of many more details than will fit in the story, the narrative approach involves a considerable amount of editing. Details of the event are reduced and organized by the author so that the story can be read in a reasonable amount of time and have

Historical narrative is the most commonly used genre in the Bible.

the intended impact on its readers. This is not to say that the biblical authors distort the details of the event; however, they do condition our experience of the event in a number of ways, including organization of the details into a plot, strategic presentation of characters, and comments made by the narrator.

The inspired authors of the Bible organize their narratives into plots; by examining these plots, we can come to a better understanding of how the author intends for us to respond to the events in the story. The plot in most Bible stories consists of several standard components: crisis, complication, climax, and resolution. The crisis typically centers on a problem that inhibits the advance of God's kingdom or a problem faced by people living in every age. Once the crisis has been introduced, the author may report on circumstances that complicate the crisis and lead to a climax. At this point, God speaks or acts, either directly or via one of His earthly representatives, to resolve the matter. This carefully organized plot pattern helps maintain the reader's attention and directs it to the enduring lesson, a lesson that will be linked to the crisis resolution in the story.

The plot in most Bible stories consists of several standard components: crisis, complication, climax, and resolution.

Bible stories can cover many pages, but we will consider a brief story from Matthew 8 to illustrate the way in which a plot looks.

Then he [Jesus] got into the boat and his disciples followed him. Suddenly a furious storm came up on the lake, so that the waves swept over the boat. But Jesus was sleeping. The disciples went and woke him, saying, "Lord, save us! We're going to drown!"

He replied, "You of little faith, why are you so afraid?" Then he got up and rebuked the winds and the waves, and it was completely calm.

The men were amazed and asked, "What kind of man is this? Even the winds and the waves obey him!" (Matthew 8:23–27).

In a short story like this, the crisis is introduced quickly. An unexpected and violent windstorm unleashes its force against a boat full of men. The crisis is further complicated by the fact that Jesus is sleeping and by the words of the disciples, who give voice to their fear of drowning. The climax is reached when Jesus rises, rebukes the weather, and removes the threat. The disciples' rhetorical question—"What kind of man is this?"—directs us to the point of the narrative: As the Son of God, Jesus is capable of addressing threats to His people with a power that is truly out of this world.

Poetry

The poetry we read in the Bible flows from real-life events, but the authors of poetic passages typically spend more time directing our attention to the ideas behind the event than on the details of the event itself. The poet presents these ideas using an extreme economy of words, which changes the appearance of the communication on the page. Rather than long paragraphs, we find short lines filled with complex grammatical patterns, embellished with colorful imagery, filled with emotion, and embroidered with a variety of literary devices. In Psalm 1, for example, the inspired poet reflects on the great fortune enjoyed by one in the Lord's care. But rather than simply tell a narrative story, the poet turns the idea into images.

Rather than simply tell a narrative story, the poet turns the idea into images.

That person is like a tree
planted by streams of water,
which yields its fruit in season
and whose leaf does not wither—
whatever they do prospers.
PSALM 1:3

The nature of poetry changes the way we read it. While historical narrative encourages us to press on quickly from crisis to resolution so that we can discover the point or outcome of the story, poetry artfully presents an idea early in the poem and calls for us to stop and reflect almost as soon as we have begun. This type of reading calls for us to slow down, turn off life's distractions, and focus our thinking on the idea the poet wishes to share.

It will help our reading of biblical poetry to understand how the ancient Hebrews composed their poetry.

It will help our reading of biblical poetry to understand how the ancient Hebrews composed their poetry. Rather than using rhyme as a primary tool, they were more apt to employ repetition, contrast, and parallel structure to develop their ideas, using combinations of two or three short lines. At times the poet uses the second line of poetry to repeat and therefore emphasize the idea of the first line. Consider this poetic call to action from the Psalms:

> *Who will rise up for me against the wicked?*
> *Who will take a stand for me*
> *against evildoers?*
> PSALM 94:16

The biblical poets may also urge our consideration of an idea by using the second line in contrast to the first. In Psalm 1 the primary idea of God's care is contrasted with the experience of the wicked.

> *For the LORD watches over the way*
> *of the righteous,*
> *but the way of the wicked leads*
> *to destruction.*
> PSALM 1:6

A third way the initial idea can be developed is by introducing the idea in the first line and then expanding it in the following lines of poetry.

> *Blessed is the one*
> *who does not walk in step*
> *with the wicked*
> *or stand in the way that sinners take*
> *or sit in the company of mockers.*
> PSALM 1:1

Recognizing that bad company can corrupt a good person, the inspired poet invites God's people to consider the company they keep and the level of contact they maintain with those who oppose the Lord. The three verbs used in these three poetic lines describe a progressive association, from "walking" to "standing" to "sitting." The blessed person avoids not only the most sustained contact with bad company—sitting—but even the most casual: walking.

These are just a few of the many patterns and literary devices in the poet's toolbox. Practice and sustained reading of biblical poetry will help us discover even more of these literary conventions. The key is to read slowly, reread, and observe the artful ways in which the poet presents, emphasizes, and develops an idea for our reflection.

> *Practice and sustained reading of biblical poetry will help us discover even more of these literary conventions.*

Law

In stark contrast to poetry, laws in the Bible are presented in straightforward language without literary adornment. The laws in the Bible directly call the people of God to holiness. They directly summon us to consider our relationship to God, to other people, and to the natural environment in which we live.

In some ways reading law is easier than reading historical narrative or poetry; but one challenge that modern Bible readers face is how to determine whether the directives we find in the Law are time limited or universally applicable. Many of the laws found in the Old Testament represent God's will for a specific period of history. For example, in an earlier era, God clearly regulated the diet of the Israelites by prohibiting the consumption of pork (see Leviticus 11:7). In the New Testament era, following the death of Jesus, this command was no longer in force (see Acts 10:9–23). One can now be holy and still have pork for dinner. By contrast, certain laws pertain to everyone down through the ages. For example, God prohibits stealing, whether we live in the twenty-first century AD or the fourteenth century BC (see Deuteronomy 5:19).

Many of the laws found in the Old Testament represent God's will for a specific period of history.

Other cases are a bit more complex because we find a law meant to apply to all time presented in language of an earlier era. Consider the following directive, which calls for a weekly day of rest: "Observe the

Sabbath day by keeping it holy, as the LORD your God has commanded you. Six days you shall labor and do all your work, but the seventh day is a sabbath to the LORD your God. On it you shall not do any work, neither you, nor your son or daughter, nor your male or female servant, nor your ox, your donkey or any of your animals, nor any foreigner residing in your towns, so that your male and female servants may rest, as you do" (Deuteronomy 5:12–14). Though we may not have servants or donkeys to help us maintain our homes, and we may not raise our own food, we can find a principle in this directive that applies universally to all time. God calls for us to set aside one day a week and free it from the mundane tasks that normally fill our days. The Jewish Sabbath was on Saturday, a day that most Christians no longer observe as Sabbath. Nevertheless, the principle of resting one day a week

God calls for us to set aside one day a week and free it from the mundane tasks that normally fill our days.

endures. To understand this genre of biblical communication, we again need to look for the controlling idea in the Law and determine if and how it applies to us in our era.

Prophecy

The prophets were God's selected representatives who were directed to speak to Old Testament Israel on God's behalf. In some cases the Lord intended for these individuals to write down their message and preserve it for future generations to read. These became the prophetic books that are named after the individual prophets—Isaiah, Jeremiah, Jonah, Haggai, and so on. We might expect such books to be filled with predictions about the future—and in some cases we do find language that speaks of a coming Messiah and a new, trouble-free age. But in most cases the prophetic writers were charged with responding to their immediate circumstances, often criticizing the

In most cases the prophetic writers were charged with responding to their immediate circumstances.

attitudes and behaviors of their audience and illustrating the relationship between their habits and their distressed circumstances. When God's people repented, the prophets were quick to offer their listeners the hope that flows from a forgiving God.

Several strategies will allow us to read the prophetic books in a more informed way. First of all, most were written in poetic form. This means that the rules for reading and interpreting poetry apply here. By using poetry, the prophets show that their emphasis is often more on an idea than an event. Our goal as readers is to find the controlling idea, examine the artful way in which the poet repeats and develops it, and reflect on its application in our lives. Because the prophets most often write in response to certain historical events, it is also helpful for us to become aware of the historical circumstances behind their writing, so that we can set their ideas in the context of the events that surround them. Early in most of the prophetic books, we find some clues as to the particular era in which the message was given, if not the specific circumstances that motivated it. We can then turn to the companion portions of historical narrative, where we might learn more about the context that gave birth to the prophetic lesson we are reading. Finally, it is helpful to read larger segments of the prophetic books in one sitting, if not the entire book itself. Because the prophetic authors frequently repeat the controlling ideas, we may find that segments of the book that seem less clear may become clearer within the context of the whole.

It is helpful to read larger segments of the prophetic books in one sitting.

Take the prophet Amos as an example. The first verses of his book help to situate the prophet in a very specific time frame (see Amos 1:1). Reading the companion historical narrative from 2 Kings and 2 Chronicles suggests that this was a more prosperous time economically for God's people, but also a time of greater idolatry and a time when the advantaged members of society were taking advantage of the disadvantaged.

Amos lays bare the problem and the consequences to come:

> *This is what the Lord says:*
> *"For three sins of Israel,*
> *even for four, I will not relent.*
> *They sell the innocent for silver,*
> *and the needy for a pair of sandals.*
> *They trample on the heads of the poor*
> *as on the dust of the ground*
> *and deny justice to the oppressed. . . .*
> *"Now then, I will crush you*
> *as a cart crushes when loaded*
> *with grain."*
> AMOS 2:6–7, 13

With words like these, Amos highlighted the social injustice rampant in the land, built the case against God's people, spoke of a coming invasion by Assyria that represented God's judgment against Israel, and then announced divine restoration, which would follow when God's people made the appropriate changes.

> *"In that day I will restore
> David's fallen shelter—
> I will repair its broken walls
> and restore its ruins—
> and will rebuild it as it used to be."*
> AMOS 9:11

Letters

The apostolic letters (or epistles) are the New Testament's counterpart to the Old Testament's prophetic books. These letters were written either by those taught directly by Jesus or by students of those taught directly by Jesus. In the months and years following Christ's death and resurrection, the Christian church expanded in all geographical directions. As it did, it ran up against new cultures and new ideologies, which led to new challenges and new questions. The letters were written to address those challenges and questions.

In contrast to the prophetic books of the Old Testament, the letters of the New Testament are composed of the kind of grammar we might use in our own correspondence—direct declarative sentences with limited use of poetry or other literary devices. In many cases we find a sense of urgency that calls for the message to get quickly and directly into the lives of God's people. But like the prophetic writers, the writers of the epistles often presume that the reader knows the circumstances that motivate the communication. Fortunately, we have the book of Acts available, in which we can find historical narrative reporting on the growth of the Christian church. Also, as with reading the Law, we need to watch for clues that help us determine which principles are applicable for all time and which apply only to the local situation and the immediate cultural circumstances of the original readers of the letters.

The letters of the New Testament are composed of the kind of grammar we might use in our own correspondence.

A passage from Galatians will illustrate

the point. This letter was written by the apostle Paul to a group of Christians in what today is southern Turkey, who had come to know Christ or learned more about Him during an earlier visit by Paul (see Acts 13:14–14:23). Though many came to believe in Jesus and celebrated the news that Paul brought, the gospel message was also met by verbal objection and physical mistreatment of the messengers. Paul wrote Galatians after his visit to the area because a subsequent group of teachers claiming a higher authority had contradicted his core message. In the letter Paul barely pauses for a civil greeting before lashing out at this new teaching: "I am astonished that you are so quickly deserting the one who called you to live in the grace of Christ and are turning to a different gospel—which is really no gospel at all. Evidently some people are

We need to watch for clues that help us determine which principles are applicable for all time and which apply only to the local situation.

throwing you into confusion and are trying to pervert the gospel of Christ" (Galatians 1:6–7). The remainder of the letter seeks to restore a proper understanding of the gospel, reaffirming the free and full forgiveness of sins offered by God through Jesus as a gift for everyone who believes. So, while it is a letter with an application targeted for a specific time and place, it also stands as a manifesto of the Christian gospel, which continues to inform and encourage us today.

Apocalyptic

Apocalyptic writing, the final genre of literature we will consider, may be the most challenging to read. Though the book of Revelation offers the most sustained use of this particular writing style, we find it in the Old Testament, as well, particularly in the second portion of Daniel. These inspired authors used this style of writing to address the

Apocalyptic writing may be the most challenging to read.

future of the world, the fate of God's people in the face of attacks by those who oppose the Lord, the return of Jesus Christ to judge the world, and the nature of the eternal kingdom that Jesus will establish. What makes this type of literature more difficult to understand is the writing style, which paints the pages of our Bible with fantastic images and extended visual metaphors, all of which move against a brightly colored and surreal backdrop. Consider the following snapshot from Revelation 13:

> Then I saw a second beast, coming out of the earth. It had two horns like a lamb, but it spoke like a dragon. It exercised all the authority of the first beast on its behalf, and made the earth and its inhabitants worship the first beast, whose fatal wound had been healed. And it performed great signs, even causing fire to come down from heaven to the earth in full view of the people. . . . It also forced all people, great and small, rich and poor, free and slave, to receive a mark on their

right hands or on their foreheads, so
that they could not buy or sell unless
they had the mark, which is the name
of the beast or the number of its name.
This calls for wisdom. Let the person
who has insight calculate the number of
the beast, for it is the number of a man.
That number is 666.
REVELATION 13:11–13, 16–18

What do the images represent? What do they teach us that can be applied to our lives as we manage our personal challenges and look toward tomorrow? Because these portions of scripture were often written against the backdrop of persecution, it is helpful to learn what we can about the historical circumstances

It is helpful to learn what we can about the historical circumstances that motivated the writing.

that motivated the writing. Only with that background in view can we take on the task of correctly decoding the images. As intriguing as the apocalyptic literature can be, newcomers to reading the Bible should probably wait until they have become more seasoned in other portions of scripture before tackling these more challenging segments of God's Word.

Within the confines of this longer chapter, we have been able to engage the topic of genre only at a fundamental level. But I trust you have become aware of its value. Though one page of the Bible can look very similar to the next, to best understand what God is saying to us in His Word, we must first determine how He is speaking.

What Is Going On behind the Scenes?

Without context, effective communication can be hopelessly impaired. Consider the following story in that light:

> A young girl left home, rushing forward as quickly as her legs would carry her. After running for a short distance, she turned left, waving her arms wildly. She turned sharply to the left and then dodged left again. Approaching home, her eyes grew big as she came face-to-face with a woman wearing a dark mask.

It is highly unlikely that the vocabulary or the grammar used in telling this brief story prove to be an obstacle to understanding. Nevertheless, you may be unable to make much sense of the story until it is put in context. These sentences describe the scene at my daughter's softball game after she hit a fly ball to deep center field.

What is going on? Sometimes our struggle to understand a portion of the Bible or our failure to fully grasp what a biblical author is saying, relates to the fact that we lack details from the historical context. In this chapter we will explore this obstacle to understanding, offer a pathway to overcome it, and illustrate how a greater understanding of historical context can deepen our engagement with the message in God's Word.

The Obstacle

There is always more going on behind the scenes in the biblical world than the authors of the Bible directly report to us. In some ways this is a good thing. Too much information can overwhelm us and distract from the important points.

Too much information can overwhelm us and distract from the important points.

If all the details of an

event were included in every Bible story, we would soon find ourselves drowning in those details and struggling to trace the contours of the plot. Likewise, if more context details were added to a piece of poetry, it would defeat the simple elegance of the poet's presentation. Nevertheless, we find many instances in which background knowledge related to the political, social, or economic circumstances surrounding a set of verses is assumed by the biblical author. Without sufficient information, our understanding of a poetic verse or a Bible story can be dramatically impaired.

We find many instances in which background knowledge. . . surrounding a set of verses is assumed by the biblical author.

The death of King Josiah provides a helpful example. This ruler of God's people inherited a kingdom that had wandered far and wide from God's plan for the nation of Israel. As a reforming king, Josiah worked aggressively and tirelessly to repair the temple and to reanimate holy living among his subjects. This earned him a remarkable accolade from God: "Neither before nor after Josiah was there a king like him who turned to the LORD as he did—with all his heart and with all his soul and with all his strength, in accordance with all the Law of Moses" (2 Kings 23:25). The account of Josiah's death is not merely noted in scripture, but is punctuated by the tragic circumstances that surrounded it. At age thirty-nine, with so much more to offer, King Josiah picked an unnecessary fight with Necho, an Egyptian king, and died in battle.

Why was Necho marching north to Carchemish to engage in a battle on the side of the Assyrians?

Even though Josiah's death is recorded in two books of the Bible (2 Kings 23:29–30 and 2 Chronicles 35:20–24), his death notice comes unexpectedly and we struggle to fully grasp what happened. Why was Necho marching north to Carchemish to engage in a battle on the side of the Assyrians? Why did Josiah engage in such a high-stakes venture, marching out against a much larger Egyptian army when the Egyptians had made it clear that their fight was not with Israel? Without answers to these questions, Bible readers cannot fully understand the death of this very important biblical figure, and we're left a bit uncertain about what lessons to draw from it.

The Solution

The solution to this challenge involves learning more about historical context. Though this may require us to leave the pages of the Bible; it does not require us to leave the story of God's interaction with the world. That's because all history, whether recorded in the Bible or not, is part of "His story." The God of the Bible is not just aware of history; He directs it. He makes history happen the way it does in order to accomplish the goals He has in mind for the world.

"Remember the former things, those of long ago; I am God, and there is no other; I am God, and there is none like

me. I make known the end from the
beginning, from ancient times, what
is still to come. I say: 'My purpose will
stand, and I will do all that I please.'
From the east I summon a bird of
prey; from a far-off land, a man to
fulfill my purpose. What I have said,
that I will bring about; what I have
planned, that I will do."
ISAIAH 46:9–11

History is driven by God's divine purpose. Though His purpose is opposed by unseen spiritual forces (see Daniel 10:12–13), history happens as God intends. This includes everything from the massive to the mundane, from the building of a reservoir (see Isaiah 22:11) to the defeat of an empire that is blocking the advance of the divine kingdom (see Isaiah 37:26). In some cases this divine plan for history is articulated in great detail, as in Daniel 7–12. But in most cases Bible readers must turn to other resources in order to collect the necessary background information unreported in the Bible. Even if history not recorded in the Bible has an important connection to the divine plan, God is either formally sponsoring the action or tolerating the events that combine to accomplish the larger goals He has in mind.

As Bible readers we can make good use of historical background information from extrabiblical sources. Ancient historians and artists collected information of past events and preserved it in their artwork and written reports. Sometimes these reports and other artifacts are nearly contemporary with the events mentioned in the Bible. Other historical records associated with biblical events date to later centuries, but all earlier than the modern era. Of course none of this information was recorded by divine inspiration, so we do not grant these sources the same level of authority as reporting found in the Bible. Nevertheless, these extrabiblical accounts

As Bible readers we can make good use of historical background information from extrabiblical sources.

reveal God's work in the world and offer valuable historical background that can improve our understanding of what the Bible says.

Illustrations

The Death of King Josiah

Let's consider two narratives, one from the Old Testament and one from the New Testament, that illustrate the value of asking and answering the question, "What is going on behind the scenes?" The first story is one I've already mentioned—the untimely death of King Josiah. To understand what happens, we need to start with the big picture. Throughout much of the Old Testament, three national superpowers— Egypt, Assyria, and Babylon—cast their shadows over events and are mentioned frequently by the biblical authors. During the thousands of years encompassed by the Old Testament, these three nations experienced times of great national strength as well as times of economic and military weakness. They also contended among themselves to control the wealth and natural resources of territories outside their borders, including the strategic, natural land bridge inhabited by the Israelites.

The story of Josiah's death occurs late in the seventh century BC as an important change was occurring on the world's stage. The Assyrians, who had built an empire from the Persian Gulf to the Red Sea, were in a state of steady decline, slowly collapsing under pressure from the rising tide of the Neo-Babylonian Empire. With their heartland and capital city lost, the Assyrians were making one last bold stand near the city of Carchemish on the Euphrates River.

To understand what happens, we need to start with the big picture.

As Pharaoh Necho of Egypt and King Josiah of Judah sized up the situation, they perceived these evolving events differently. The Egyptians were pleased to have the Assyrians and Babylonians fighting each other to the point of physical and economic exhaustion. This opened the door for Egypt to fill the vacuum created when these two competitors had weakened one another. When Necho saw that Assyria was increasingly on the ropes, he developed a plan to prop up the flagging Assyrians by rolling Egyptian soldiers toward Carchemish. Josiah, meanwhile, had a different perspective. God's people, who had experienced a violent invasion and occupation of their land at the hands of Assyria, were happy to see the weakened empire on the brink of collapse. The other regional power, Babylon, was much farther east than Assyria, and Josiah may have hoped that the Babylonians would not seek to exert their influence over Israel, at least in the near future.

The Assyrians were making one last bold stand near the city of Carchemish on the Euphrates River.

These details, gleaned from extrabiblical sources, help us understand why Necho was marching north to Carchemish to engage in a battle on the side of the Assyrians. His goal was to pass quickly through the territory of Judah on his way to assist the Assyrians at Carchemish, so that the Egyptians might take advantage of continuing hostilities between Assyria and Babylon. Why then did Josiah engage in such a high-stakes venture, marching out against the Egyptian army, when Necho had made it clear to him that Egypt's fight was not with Judah? Josiah's goal was to interrupt and delay the arrival of the Egyptian reinforcements so that Babylon might finish off the last vestiges of the Assyrian military resistance at Carchemish. In doing so he believed that his own kingdom would be preserved.

Understanding the historical background and the general role that God plays in history allows us to get the point of this brief narrative.

Understanding the historical background and the general role that God plays in history allows us to get the point of this brief narrative. It is not just that Josiah died, but that he died as a consequence of making a grave theological error. Despite his remarkable record of reformation and drawing the people of Judah back to God, Josiah's actions now put him in conflict with God's purposes. The Lord had planned for the Babylonians to defeat the Assyrians at Carchemish. He had also allowed for Egyptian involvement in this battle, though their presence would not change the outcome. Even though Necho had made his plans clear to Josiah (see 2 Chronicles 35:21), Josiah chose to rely on his own perception and his ability to manipulate world events. The story offers a stunning warning to everyone tempted to follow Josiah's lead. "He [Josiah] would not listen to what Necho had said at God's command but went to fight him on the plain of Megiddo" (2 Chronicles 35:22). No matter how well intentioned we might be, we cannot change God's plans, only live within

We cannot change God's plans, only live within them.

them. Josiah paid for his act of hubris with his life.

The Verdict of Pontius Pilate

A second story that illustrates the value of historical background comes from the New Testament. It is the story of how the Jewish religious leaders manipulated Pontius Pilate, the Roman governor at the time of Jesus' arrest and trial. The interaction between the Jewish leaders, Jesus, and Pilate are recorded in all four Gospels (see Matthew 27:11–26; Mark 15:2–15; Luke 23:1–25; and John 18:29–19:16). But despite the attention paid by the biblical writers to these events, we are still missing a key piece of information that would allow us to answer an important question: Why did Pilate, the man holding the most powerful political position in the story, succumb to the pressure of the Jewish leaders and ultimately condemn an innocent man to die?

When Jesus confronted the local religious establishment of His day, whose leaders had been thoroughly corrupted, He picked a fight with a group of men who had a lot to lose and who were experienced in fighting for position and power. The aristocratic priests of Jerusalem stood to lose professionally, socially, and economically under Jesus' unrelenting criticism of their character and behavior. What is more, these wealthy politicians had been hardened by their negotiations with Rome and were of no mind to concede a single point to the upstart teacher from Galilee.

So why did the powerful governor yield to pressure as he did?

They wanted to be rid of Jesus, but they did not want to dirty their own hands with the deed, so they set about executing a plan that would involve the Roman governor, Pontius Pilate. The charges the Jewish leaders brought against Jesus were serious. They claimed He was leading a movement to overthrow the Roman occupation of Judea. However, during Jesus' trial the charges collapsed in the face of the evidence, and Pilate appropriately pronounced Jesus' innocence. That is how the story should have ended; so why did the powerful governor yield to pressure as he did?

The answer lies both in Pilate's position and the political realities that undercut him. During the time of Jesus, the nation of Israel was under the control of Rome. This included the region of Judea and the city of Jerusalem. The man in charge of collecting the taxes and keeping the peace in that part of the Roman world was the Roman-appointed governor, Pontius Pilate. He was neither the first nor the last such governor, but he was the man in charge during the final years of Jesus' life on earth. Pilate's duties included those

The answer lies both in Pilate's position and the political realities that undercut him.

we associate with the executive branch of government, but they also extended into the judicial realm. He was, in effect, the Supreme Court justice. In the absence of a jury, he entertained the charges, heard the evidence, and issued the verdict. What is more, the only one empowered to overturn his verdict was the Roman emperor himself. During Jesus' trial, when Jesus did not immediately respond to the questions directed His way by Pilate, the Roman judge said, "Don't you realize I have power either to free you or to crucify you?" (John 19:10).

In many ways, Pilate had it right—which makes it all the more surprising to see justice go so horribly wrong when the Jewish leaders manipulate him into issuing a verdict he does not really own. But here is the background information that allows us to make more sense of these events. Pilate had come into office in AD 26, the fifth Roman governor over Judea since AD 6. His tenure in office was marked repeatedly by insensitivity to the cultures that he governed and by heartless cruelty against those he ruled. Josephus, the first-century historian, makes note of a number of such instances. For example, Pilate confiscated money from the temple treasury to pay for a

Here is the background information that allows us to make more sense of these events.

new water-delivery system he was building for Jerusalem. And the Bible itself recalls an instance in which Pilate massacred Galileans who had come to worship at the temple in Jerusalem (see Luke 13:1–2).

Because Rome was far away from Judea, as long as the news of these abuses remained a local story, Pilate was unconcerned. But there was one thing that struck fear into the governor's heart: the prospect of Jewish citizens traveling to Rome to deliver a personal report on Pilate's misconduct. Here the Jewish historian Philo offers a crucial insight: "It was this final point which particularly exasperated him [Pilate], for he feared that if they actually sent an embassy, they would also expose the rest of his conduct as governor by stating in full the briberies, the insults, the robberies, the outrages and wanton injuries, the executions without trial constantly repeated, the ceaseless and supremely grievous cruelty" (Philo, *Embassy*

> *As long as the news of these abuses remained a local story, Pilate was unconcerned.*

of Gauis, paragraph 38). In the end, after the death and resurrection of Jesus, it was just this kind of report, delivered by the Samaritans, that resulted in Pilate's being recalled to Rome.

The Jewish leaders were well aware of Pilate's vulnerabilities and were quick to exploit them. When they sought to involve the governor in condemning Jesus, they played heavily on that fear to manipulate the verdict. At times the threat to send an embassy to report on Pilate

Without context, effective communication is often hopelessly impaired.

was subtle, and at other times it was made very public—particularly when they were afraid that Pilate was about to release Jesus. They shouted as one, "If you let this man go, you are no friend of Caesar. Anyone who claims to be a king opposes Caesar" (John 19:12). The Jewish leaders put their finger on the one thing Pilate feared, and that is how they were able to manipulate this powerful Roman governor into issuing the desired verdict against Jesus.

Without context, effective communication is often hopelessly impaired. To deepen our understanding of God's Word, we can legitimately ask, "What is going on behind the scenes?" As we work to answer that question, we honor the fact that all history is part of God's story, and we tap into a storehouse of information that provides essential background for understanding God's Word.

What Are They Doing?

People of every age and location have unique cultural practices that leave outsiders scratching their heads and asking, "What are they doing?" Milwaukee, Wisconsin, is no exception. If you come to this city's beaches on January 1, you will see what I mean. Each year on this date, hundreds of people mill about on the Lake Michigan shoreline dressed in a wide variety of attire, from traditional swimwear to Green Bay Packers uniforms to three-piece business suits. Around noon this diverse group heads as one for the water. Some walk, most run, and a few daring souls ride their bikes toward the waves. No matter how they get there, the goal is the same: to take the first swim of the year in Lake Michigan. What is shocking is to realize that the water temperature is around 38 degrees and the outside air temperature might be in the teens—not counting windchill. The event is aptly named the Polar Bear Plunge.

There is no swimming in freezing water in the Bible, but as Bible readers we are certain to encounter cultural practices from the past that may amuse us and confuse us. In this chapter we will consider this category of misunderstanding, discuss how the mystery can be removed, and illustrate how a deeper understanding of ancient culture can advance our understanding of God's Word.

As Bible readers we are certain to encounter cultural practices from the past that may amuse us and confuse us.

The Obstacle

What are they doing? Because the Bible was written by people living in the past about people who were going about the normal routines of daily life in that era and location, we can expect to encounter ancient cultural practices in our Bible reading. On the one hand, many of the day-to-day activities mentioned in the Bible strike a familiar chord. The human experience is the human experience, whether we lived two thousand years before the time of Christ or in the twenty-first century of the modern era. In a typical week, people everywhere do similar sorts of things—make and wear clothing, build and occupy homes, secure a supply of fresh water, and provide their families with food. People everywhere go to work, travel, and relax.

These points of continuity in the human experience help us connect with cultures across the world and throughout history.

These points of continuity in the human experience help us connect with cultures across the world and throughout history.

The challenge comes when we read about cultural practices that are foreign to our experience. For example, when we want a drink of water, we walk to the kitchen faucet or the refrigerator. In the ancient world, however, the story was very different. A drink of water came from a well or a cistern, which was dug by members of the family. Maintenance and defense of this water resource was a constant concern and occupied hours of time in any given week.

The same differences are apparent when we think about the bread we use to make our lunches. For most of us, bread comes from the local grocery store. In the ancient world, enjoying daily bread was the end of a yearlong process that involved plowing fields, planting, weeding, harvesting the grain, processing the grain into flour, and baking the bread for daily use.

We often find unique cultural practices mentioned in narrative accounts.

In the Bible we often find unique cultural practices mentioned in narrative accounts. For example, the digging and defending of a well is at center stage in an episode from Abraham's life. A well that Abraham had dug at Beersheba is seized by a neighboring clan. Confrontation, negotiation, and a treaty ceremony become part of Abraham's story as this water rights issue is addressed (see Genesis 21:25–31). In the New Testament, a Samaritan village well becomes the centerpiece of a story from Jesus' life as He engages a woman from the village of Sychar in a conversation about water that turns into a conversation about His identity as the Messiah (see John 4:4–9).

We also find cultural practices used as metaphors in the Bible. For example, God's criticism of His chosen people is packaged in image-laden language: "My people have committed two sins: They have forsaken me, the spring of living water, and have dug their own cisterns, broken cisterns that cannot hold water" (Jeremiah 2:13). In the New Testament, Jesus cautions His disciples

We also find cultural practices used as metaphors in the Bible.

about becoming lax in their life's witness by employing the image of salt: "Salt is good, but if it loses its saltiness, how can it be made salty again? It is fit neither for the soil nor for the manure pile; it is thrown out. Whoever has ears to hear, let them hear" (Luke 14:34-36). We have ears with which to hear, but we do not have manure piles into which we throw salt! So we are left to ask, "What is going on here?" When cultural images foreign to our experience are introduced by the biblical writers, they can become obstacles to understanding.

When cultural images foreign to our experience are introduced by the biblical writers, they can become obstacles to understanding.

The Solution

It can be more than a little difficult to keep up with the contemporary twists and turns of our own culture. We are met by a growing list of changes to master, whether that is new software on our computer, a new car that parallel parks itself, or a cell phone that acts more like a computer than a phone. That is to say nothing of the clothing and diet fads that seem to change weekly in our world. There is plenty of work to do in keeping up with our own changing culture without adding the burden of learning about ancient cultures. But for Bible readers the extra energy expended is worth the effort.

In light of the many recent discoveries in archaeology, it is now possible to immerse ourselves in a deeper understanding of ancient culture. Scholars continue to unearth fresh and exciting insights into the cultures of the past. Today we know more than ever about past practices such as betrothal and marriage, agriculture, and warfare. We also know more about the tools of ancient culture, such as grain mills, city gates, and olive presses. When we carry these insights into our study of the Bible, we will see things we had not seen before and will understand passages that once left us confused. The following illustrations demonstrate the value of cultural insight in our pursuit of deeper biblical understanding.

It is now possible to immerse ourselves in a deeper understanding of ancient culture.

Illustrations

We can illustrate the value of becoming more culturally aware by briefly discussing ancient practices associated with cisterns, signet rings, betrothal, mangers, and salt.

Cistern

Israel is a land with precious few natural resources and a real shortage of freshwater. With the scarcity of freshwater lakes or rivers in the region, the freshwater used by those living in the Promised Land during Bible times was well water and rainwater. Gathering rainwater was relatively easy during the rainy months, but during the five months of the year when little or no rain fell, it was necessary to tap into the supply of rainwater that had fallen weeks or months earlier. One way to do this was with a cistern, which in ancient Israel was an underground water-storage chamber dug into the limestone and plastered annually to keep it from leaking. On

Israel is a land with precious few natural resources and a real shortage of freshwater.

rainy days the surface runoff was directed into the cisterns, which varied in size depending on whether they were meeting the needs of a city or a single household. In cross-section, most cisterns have a bell-like shape with a narrow neck that connects the storage chamber with the earth's surface. The water entered the cistern and was drawn from the cistern through that neck.

The Bible mentions cisterns on several occasions. Some of these are associated with cities; others were dug in the countryside to provide water for grazing livestock (see 2 Chronicles 26:10). The unique design of a cistern made it an ideal place to imprison someone you wanted to detain. When Joseph's brothers chose to keep him in custody while determining his fate, they put him in a cistern (see Genesis 37:21–24). And those who found the prophet Jeremiah's message unwelcome detained him the same way (see Jeremiah 38:6).

Ironically, the book that bears Jeremiah's name employs the cistern as a metaphor to describe the poor choices that God's people had made. In spite of the constant care God had shown the Israelites, they had repeatedly violated the first commandment, turning their backs on the Lord while investing themselves in the worship of other gods. This behavior was so unthinkable it required illustration: "My people have committed two sins: They have forsaken me, the spring of living water, and have dug their own cisterns, broken cisterns that cannot hold water" (Jeremiah 2:13). To understand the metaphor, we need to understand the difference between water obtained from a spring and water obtained from a cistern; both are supplied by rainwater, but in very different ways. Rain absorbed by the soil trickles down to the water table. In most places, the water table is below the surface of the ground; but when the water table and ground level coincide in elevation, a spring breaks out, providing the most desirable water in the ancient world.

To understand the metaphor, we need to understand the difference between water obtained from a spring and water obtained from a cistern.

Such springs did not require excavation or maintenance. What is more, the springwater was naturally filtered and always fresh. By contrast, water from a cistern was not naturally filtered and often brackish. On top of that, maintaining a cistern was time and labor intensive. First there was the initial excavation, but then the cistern required regular maintenance, as well—draining, cleaning, and replastering at least once a year. Without the necessary maintenance, the cistern would leak, resulting in a loss of water. In using the metaphor of springs and cisterns in Jeremiah 2:13, the Lord assumes the people are aware of the differences between the two. He compares Himself to the highly desirable springwater that Israel had abandoned. Instead, they had turned to other deities, who are likened not just to a cistern but to a broken cistern, which is incapable of holding water. The metaphor highlights the unthinkable nature of their actions.

Signet Ring

Better understanding of the signet

ring can also deepen our understanding of God's message in the Bible. As the name suggests, the signet ring is a loop of metal, often stirruplike in shape with a flat upper surface. That upper surface is incised with a distinctive design, which when pressed into soft clay or warmed wax leaves a unique impression. A signet ring was unique to an individual, and the impression was used to mark a document as one's own, like putting a signature on an official document today.

A signet ring was unique to an individual, and the impression was used to mark a document as one's own.

We find both literal and figurative uses of signet rings in the Bible. For example, when Joseph rose in social rank from slave and prisoner to second in command of all Egypt, "Pharaoh took his signet ring from his finger and put it on Joseph's finger" (Genesis 41:42). Consider the power this gave Joseph; he now had the ability to execute the "signature" of the Egyptian ruler.

Because the signet ring was such a cherished personal possession, and because it carried the connotations of power, God uses it as a metaphor in referring to mortals who are leaders of His people. In the case of one king of Judah, the Lord expressed His displeasure over this man's leadership with these words: " 'As surely as I live,' declares the Lord, 'even if you, Jehoiachin son of Jehoiakim king of Judah, were a signet ring on my right hand, I would still pull you off' " (Jeremiah 22:24). On the other hand, the leadership of a subsequent descendant of David's is affirmed with exactly the opposite image: " 'On that day,' declares the Lord Almighty, 'I will take you, my servant Zerubbabel son of Shealtiel,' declares the Lord, 'and I will make you like my signet ring, for I have chosen you,' declares the Lord Almighty" (Haggai 2:23).

Betrothal

In American culture a ring plays a central role in a couple's engagement. Not so in the biblical world. In fact, many aspects of getting married in Israel during the first century are strikingly different from our modern experience. In a remote Jewish village like Nazareth, marriages were arranged—meaning it was the parents who identified the most desirable match for their sons and daughters, and then they made a marriage contract with the other family. Once that contract was made, the betrothal was on. It is not just the process of betrothal that sounds peculiar, but also the age of the betrothed. Evidence suggests that Jewish girls of the first century were engaged to be married when they were as young as eleven or twelve, and married by the time they were thirteen.

Many aspects of getting married in Israel during the first century are strikingly different from our modern experience.

This information can really change our perspective on Mary, the mother of Jesus. In Luke 1 we read that an angel appeared to her to announce that she was going to have a remarkable experience. The long-awaited Savior was going to enter the mortal world via her body. This child would not be the biological child of her fiancé, Joseph, but rather, she was told, "The Holy Spirit will come on you, and the power of the Most High will overshadow you. So the holy one to be born will be called the Son of God" (Luke 1:35). Soon afterward, Mary expressed her willingness to take on this responsibility, laden with challenges as it was. She now would have to defend the legitimacy of this unique pregnancy to her fiancé, her family, and her neighbors. The angel presented an assignment that would

The angel presented an assignment that would have been a challenge for any seasoned adult.

have been a challenge for any seasoned adult, given the very conservative culture in Nazareth, let alone for a girl of eleven or twelve years. With this additional knowledge, we grow in appreciation of Mary's remarkable faith and character.

Mary was not much older than twelve or thirteen when she gave birth to Jesus and placed him in a manger. All ordinary families of Jesus' day had their own animals to provide the family with meat, milk, and shelter, as well as the capacity to carry heavy loads, pull plows, and draw wagons. During daylight hours, it was relatively safe for the animals to be in the open country. But at night, when large predators roamed the fields, the animals were brought into the family living compound for safekeeping. The food they ate was placed in a feedbox or manger. Such mangers were about as functional in material and design as they could be. A typical manger was about three feet long and three feet tall. It could be carved out of limestone, or more often, shaped out of compacted mud and clay. Of all the places in the ancient world we might look for decoration and

A typical manger was about three feet long and three feet tall.

elegance, this was not it. The ordinary manger was simple in form, utilitarian, and undecorated.

You may know that Jesus was placed in a manger shortly after His birth. But did you know that this fact is mentioned again and again for the sake of emphasis in the Christmas story? It is mentioned three times in the account of Jesus' birth (see Luke 2:7, 12, 16). And the manger is identified as a "sign" when the angel speaks to the Christmas shepherds. "This will be a sign to you: You will find a baby wrapped in cloths and lying in a manger" (Luke 2:12). For Luke a "sign" is always an image that carries special meaning. An animal feeding trough was no place for a baby, much less a baby who had been identified as royalty, much less the anticipated King of the world who would rule an eternal kingdom. The manger is emphasized in Luke because it offers an insight into how this divine King would rule. He would not rule the world with the arrogance displayed by so many mortal kings. This would be a humble king. And long before we hear Jesus say it, the manger sends the following message: "The Son of Man did not come to be served, but to serve, and to give his life as a ransom for many" (Matthew 20:28).

Salt

Salt is something we know about. We enjoy putting at least a pinch of salt on our food to improve its flavor. Those living in the days of Jesus did the same thing. However. the ancients would not have recognized the small white grains of nearly pure sodium chloride found in our saltshakers. For those living in Bible times, saltcame to the table in chunks; and those chunks were anything but pure salt. A chunk of salt used to season food was actually composed of pure salt, soil, and other impurities that either lacked taste or carried a bitter taste. To get some of the more desirable salt from that

For those living in Bible times, salt came to the table in chunks.

chunk, it was necessary to pound it on the table or floor to flake off some of the pure salt. Over time this process would leave a person with a chunk of material that contained a whole lot more by-product than salt—salt that had lost its saltiness, if you will. A chunk of salt in this condition was no longer valuable for seasoning food, nor was it worth throwing into the family manure pile.

That last point requires some explanation. People in Bible times had to build fires both for cooking meals and for keeping warm during the colder winter months. Because there was a shortage of timber in the Promised Land, those fires were most often kindled with grasses, brush, and manure. Families gathered the manure left behind by their animals, moistened it, and added salt. Because this salted manure burned at a higher temperature, it produced a more efficient fire for cooking a meal or heating a home.

Jesus seized upon this imagery when discussing the important role His disciples were to play in the world. The message of

Jesus had changed them so that they, in turn, might begin to change the lives of those around them. In this way, they had become like salt, capable of improving those whose lives they touched. However, if they retreated from the teachings of Jesus or failed to enact them in their lives, that positive influence would be lost. Jesus conveyed this message with salt imagery. "Salt is good, but if it loses its saltiness, how can it be made salty again? It is fit neither for the soil nor for the manure pile; it is thrown out" (Luke 14:34–35).

They had become like salt, capable of improving those whose lives they touched.

As we have seen, it is possible to understand the culture of the biblical world and learn more about the implements and practices we find in the pages of our Bibles. New and deeper understanding is sure to follow when we ask and answer the question, "What are they doing?"

Where Am I?

Whenever we leave home to explore less familiar places, getting lost is bound to happen. It's part of learning our way around—even if we have maps or an onboard GPS. Sometimes, asking for directions is the only hope we have. But asking directions from a local offers no guarantee that we won't end up feeling even more lost. Have you ever gotten directions that sounded something like this? "All you need to do is turn south at the next intersection. Keep

When the biblical authors start to mention geography, it can sound. . . impenetrable and confusing.

going until you get to the farm that Sam Jenkins gave to his grandson two years ago, and then turn east. From there it is just four miles the other side of Miller Lake. You can't miss it!" When the biblical authors start to mention geography, it can sound just about as impenetrable and confusing as that. For example, you might be familiar with the story of David and Goliath, but what are we to make of the two verses that start this familiar story? "Now the Philistines gathered their forces for war and assembled at Sokoh in Judah. They pitched camp at Ephes Dammim, between Sokoh and Azekah. Saul and the Israelites assembled and camped in the Valley of Elah" (1 Samuel 17:1–2).

Where am I? Open to just about any page in the Bible and you will find at least a few references to geography. Sometimes it will be the name of a city or region. Other times it will be a reference to terrain or rainfall. And still other pages, such as those in the latter half of Joshua, will be filled with nothing but long lists of place names that sound as peculiar to us as the street names in our local community would have sounded to someone living in Joshua's day. If we do not ignore these lists altogether, our best efforts to negotiate them can leave us exhausted and frustrated. The goal of this chapter is to take the geographical obstacle out of the way. It will help you understand why geography appears so frequently in the pages of the Bible. We will discuss how we might come to a better understanding of biblical geography and illustrate the insights we can obtain when we bring a better understanding of biblical geography to our Bible reading.

The Obstacle

Geography appears often on the pages of the Bible for three reasons. First, the Bible is filled with stories about real people who lived in real places. Knowing something about the places these people lived can help us understand more about lives and circumstances. Next, we encounter geography in our Bible reading because God has intimately linked the central message of the Bible to a place,

> *The Bible is filled with stories about real people who lived in real places.*

the Promised Land. In reading the Bible, we get no further than Genesis 12 before that connection becomes clear. Although God's creation had rebelled against Him, He was not about to abandon it. The biggest of the big ideas in the Bible is that God would send a Savior to rescue the world from its sin-ruined state. When God connected that promise to the family of Abram, He also connected it to Canaan, the Promised Land. In time the Messiah came from Abram's descendants and accomplished his saving mission in that same geographical location (see Genesis 3:1–3). From Genesis 3 on, the inspired authors of the Bible never let this detail stray far from their focus. The central message of the Bible is firmly linked to geography.

The central message of the Bible is firmly linked to geography.

The third reason that geography finds its way so frequently onto the pages of the Bible is that geography has the ability to influence our perceptions and responses. Consider the power of the phrase,

"Remember the Alamo!" This cry, used at the battle of San Jacinto in 1836, employs a place namē meant to encourage those fighting for the independence of Texas. It had the power to inspire because it was not just a place name, but a place name linked to a highly charged, emotional event. Places are not merely locations on a map; they carry connotations that the biblical authors can use to influence perception and call for action.

As the Holy Spirit guided the hands and hearts of the Bible's inspired authors, He frequently directed them to include mention of geography. Sometimes that geography appears in poetry: "As the mountains surround Jerusalem, so the LORD surrounds his people both now and forevermore" (Psalm 125:2). At other

Geography can become an obstacle to understanding.

times, it appears in familiar Bible stories, such as the story of David and Goliath. In each case, whether subtle or striking, geography can become an obstacle to understanding, because we simply are not familiar with that part of the world.

The Solution

The first step in understanding how geography can aid our understanding of the Bible is to begin to notice when we run across geographical references. Of course, that means knowing what geography is. Perhaps the first thing that comes to mind is a map. But maps are only tools that display geography. So what is geography? To make it easy, think

Again, the first step is to notice those details as you read.

in terms of two categories: the features and processes that happen on the surface of the earth (physical geography) and the way in which humans respond to those features and processes (human geography). When I read a portion of the Bible, I pay attention to mentions of geology, topography, water, climate, and forestation. I also look for the cultural responses to that geography: water acquisition, city and home construction, land use, and road building. Again, the first step is to notice those details as you read.

The second step is to learn as much as we can about the geographical items we encounter. The proper names of places like the Elah Valley, Sokoh, Shechem, or even Jerusalem will require us to become spatially oriented. A helpful place to start is with a Bible atlas, which can provide basic information on the lands of the Bible and maps to assist in your orientation. Other books written about the physical and human geography of the biblical world can help us learn more about these dimensions of the Bible. The illustrations that follow will demonstrate the value of taking such tools in hand as we read.

Illustration

The Story of David and Goliath

The story of David and Goliath begins with a rush of geographical details that most people fail to notice. "Now the Philistines gathered their forces for war and assembled at Sokoh in Judah. They pitched camp at Ephes Dammim, between Sokoh and Azekah. Saul and the Israelites assembled and camped in the Valley of Elah and drew up their battle line to meet the Philistines" (1 Samuel 17:1–2). We will do a bit of work to decode this geographical description before we consider the ways in which understanding the geography changes our reading of the narrative.

We consider the ways in which understanding the geography changes our reading of the narrative.

In the first verses of the story, the inspired author directs our attention to the Elah Valley; all the other place names (Sokoh, Azekah, Ephes Dammim) have a connection to this valley. To understand the importance of the Elah Valley is to understand the connection between geography and national security in ancient Israel. The western portion of the Promised Land that runs along the

Mediterranean Sea is an undulating plain that gently rises and falls with less than 150 feet of elevation change. This is where the Philistines lived, on the agriculturally rich and open coastal plain. By contrast the Israelites lived along the mountain spine that runs north and south through the heart of Israel. The hilly terrain of central Israel is difficult to farm, but it offers a great deal of security. Between the mountainous region where the Israelites lived and the coastal plain where the Philistines lived is a transition zone called the Shephelah. The Shephelah region is characterized by lower foothills and wide valleys. The valleys run east

The hilly terrain of central Israel is difficult to farm, but it offers a great deal of security.

and west, perpendicular to the mountains, providing a natural travel corridor from the coastal plain to the mountainous interior. To enjoy the highest level of national security, the Israelites needed to control these valleys as a buffer zone. If their chief rival, the Philistines, elected to attack, they would do so using a valley in the Shephelah. If the Israelites lost the battle in the valley, it put their homes, cities, and villages in imminent danger.

That general picture will help us decode what the author of 1 Samuel says about the circumstances on the day that David defeated Goliath. The Philistines had pitched their camp in one of the Shephelah valleys called the Elah Valley. The position of their camp is given in some detail. They were camped in Ephes Dammim between Sokoh and Azekah. This means that the Philistines had not just entered the Elah Valley but had penetrated and now controlled nearly the entire extent of it. This left King Saul and his soldiers clinging to the far eastern section of this critical valley, which had been all but lost to the Philistine invaders.

[Geographical details] will help us decode. . .about the circumstances on the day that David defeated Goliath.

How does the geography of 1 Samuel 17:1–3 shape the way we read the story of

David and Goliath? Consider first what this story is about. God had selected Saul to be the first king of Israel. His role as king was clearly defined both by his subjects and by God. His subjects expected Saul to go before them and fight their battles (see 1 Samuel 8:20). The Lord had made it clear that Israel's king was to lead the people so that they might remain faithful to God and accomplish the sacred mission of bringing the Messiah into the world (see Deuteronomy 17:14–20). Sadly, Saul failed on both counts. That is why the Lord anointed David as the king who would succeed Saul (see 1 Samuel 16).

Those details, when combined with an understanding of the geography, set the stage for the story of David and Goliath. On the one hand, political tension fills the air. Saul, the sitting king, has been rejected by God. Yet the newly anointed king has

The Lord had made it clear that Israel's king was to lead the people so that they might remain faithful to God.

not been publicly recognized or sworn into office. The political tension is driven by the question of who is to lead God's people. The geographical information given in the introduction to this story indicates that Israel is witnessing a full-blown national emergency. The Philistines have marched their armies deep into the Elah Valley and show no signs of stopping there. If there was a time for faith, if there was a time for courage, if there was a time for godly leadership, this was it.

Saul had failed to lead or inspire anything but fear in his men for more than a month.

With a political crisis and national emergency hanging in the air, we are invited to compare the ways in which Saul and David respond. Saul had failed to lead or inspire anything but fear in his men for more than a month (see 1 Samuel 17:11, 16). By contrast, David changes everything within a day of his arrival. With words and actions, he proves that he is the one with the robust faith in God and the courage that might bring security to Israel. Goliath bristled with the latest and greatest in military technology, but David had something more. "You come against me with sword and spear and javelin, but I come against you in the name of the LORD Almighty, the God of the armies of Israel, whom you have defied" (1 Samuel 17:45). In the Elah Valley, we see what we have come to expect from Saul: more weakness and failure. He does not leave the royal throne by the close of the narrative, but we leave the story even more convinced that his time is up and that David's time has come. Our impression of both leaders is informed by our understanding of the geographical location of the impending battle.

Our impression of both leaders is informed by our understanding of the geographical location of the impending battle.

The Mountains
Surrounding Jerusalem

The poetry of the Old Testament lifts our eyes from the mundane to the magnificent, from the ordinary and upsetting circumstances of life to the enduring promises of God. Yet, in lifting our eyes to the heavens, these divinely inspired poets often turn our eyes back to the earth as they search for images to convey their message. That is the case in Psalm 125, where the psalmist challenges us to see how geography has something to teach us about the magnificence of the Lord.

Those who trust in the LORD
are like Mount Zion,
which cannot be shaken but endures forever.
As the mountains surround Jerusalem,
so the LORD surrounds his people
both now and forevermore.
PSALM 125:1–2

Again, let's extract and study the geography before we consider its role in these verses. The mention of Mount Zion and Jerusalem immediately takes us to the city that had become Israel's religious and political capital (see 2 Samuel 5:6–10). At first blush we may question the logic of David's choice of Jerusalem, because the city came with a load of unappealing baggage. David's Jerusalem had a meager water supply that would support a relatively small population. The narrow valleys that surround and bisect Jerusalem offer little by way of level ground for growing food. Furthermore, the city was located some distance away from the major transportation arteries that carried the commerce of the world, so there was very little money to be made here. But the one advantage that outweighed all the negatives was security.

The security of Jerusalem has a direct link to the topography of the region. Jerusalem is buried deep in the central mountains of Israel, miles from the flat and accessible coastal plain that runs north and south

> *The security of Jerusalem has a direct link to the topography of the region.*

along the Mediterranean Sea. International armies with a mind to attack and defeat Jerusalem had quite a task before them. After arriving on the more easily traveled coastal plain, they soon found themselves picking their way east through difficult, mountainous terrain. Some routes through the mountains proved more promising travel corridors than others, but in most cases, invading armies were confronted by narrow V-shaped valleys, which put the invading soldiers in a constricted setting where fatal blows could be struck from above. The less numerous and less well-equipped Israelite soldiers were so effective at using this terrain to their advantage that many international powers never made an attempt to reach the capital city. The rewards were too small and the risk was too high to make an assault on Jerusalem worthwhile. Because the mountains that surround Jerusalem also protected it, they became synonymous with

Armies were confronted by narrow V-shaped valleys.

the security of the capital city.

The second quality of these mountains that the poet puts to work is their endurance. The mountains surrounding Jerusalem look much the same today as they did three thousand years ago. In any one lifetime, they simply do not change. They owe their longevity to their geologic composition. These mountains are composed of Cenomanian limestone, the surface of which erodes at a rate of approximately one centimeter per thousand years! At that rate, those who walk the ridges and tend the valleys never see a significant change. From a human perspective, the mountains that surround Jerusalem do not change and thus appear poised to endure forever.

From a human perspective, the mountains that surround Jerusalem do not change and thus appear poised to endure forever.

With that geography in mind, let's return to Psalm 125. This hymn of worship, along with other psalms labeled "A Song of Ascents," were traditionally used by

Jewish pilgrims who were ascending the valleys leading up to Jerusalem. Their hearts and minds were set on worshipping the Lord at His temple. These songs accompanied their steps and challenged them to see life as God sees it. In the case of Psalm 125, the opening verses celebrate the benefits gleaned by those who put their trust in the Lord. They are like the place to which they are going to worship, Mount Zion. Though perils might threaten on the coast, the capital remains unshaken because the Lord has taken up a defensive position around His people. He is, in fact, like the mountains that reach out from and surround Jerusalem.

Though the mountains will change over the course of millennia, the Lord's promise of security never changes or expires.

The security the Lord provides is not only sturdy and solid like the mountains, but it also endures like the mountains. The inspired poet reminds us not once but twice that God's people enjoy protection that endures forever. Though the mountains will change over the course of millennia, the Lord's promise of security never changes or expires. "As the mountains surround Jerusalem, so the LORD surrounds his people both now and forevermore" (Psalm 125:2).

Where am I? Open to just about any page in the Bible and you will find references to geography. Sometimes it will be the name of a city or region. Other times it will be a reference to terrain or rainfall. And there will be more than a few place names that sound as peculiar to us as the street names in our local community would have sounded to someone living in Jesus' day. Using the suggestions in this chapter, turn those quiet, unassuming, even confusing references into an opportunity to learn about the Bible's geography and how it shapes the Bible's message.

Conclusion

Do you understand what you are reading?

Although Philip, "the evangelist" of the Bible, initially directed this probing question to a well-educated man from Ethiopia, it is a question that confronts us as contemporary Bible readers, as well. The question acknowledges a reality that we know all too well: At times and in places, the Bible can be difficult to understand. So our desire to read God's Word lives in tension with the frustration we may feel when we do.

These frustrations often cause the most important book we could ever read to go unread.

These frustrations often cause the most important book we could ever read to go unread. And as our Bibles sit on the shelf collecting dust, we do without the incredible insights and the enduring comfort God desperately wants to share with us.

Fortunately this dilemma has a solution—as this book has attempted to show, the major obstacles that stand in the way of our Bible reading can be diminished. When we appreciate the unique heritage of the Bible—its divine and human sides— we find it easier to engage when scripture challenges us to believe the unbelievable and to do the unthinkable. When we re- member that while the Bible generally moves forward in time from the book of Genesis through the book of Revelation— but that it also circles back to repeat and emphasize "big ideas" that God longs to share with us—we'll be better able to follow the overall story line of scripture. When we observe changes in genre and put our minds in concert with those particular styles of writing, we will be rewarded with a more satisfying experience. And when we appreciate the historical, cultural, or geographical context of each passage, we find deepened insights into God's Word.

Do you understand what you are reading? We may never understand everything—but we will understand much more when we ask and answer the questions posed in this book: What is the Bible? What is God talking about? How is God speaking? What is going on behind the scenes? What are they doing? Where am I?

We pray that God will bless as you follow these questions down the path to deeper understanding of His Word.

With the principles of Understand Your Bible in mind, why not try reading through your Bible in a year? The following plan divides scripture into Old Testament, New Testament, and wisdom book readings that will take you 15–20 minutes a day.

Day 1	Gen. 1–2	Matt. 1	Ps. 1
Day 2	Gen. 3–4	Matt. 2	Ps. 2
Day 3	Gen. 5–7	Matt. 3	Ps. 3
Day 4	Gen. 8–10	Matt. 4	Ps. 4
Day 5	Gen. 11–13	Matt. 5:1–20	Ps. 5
Day 6	Gen. 14–16	Matt. 5:21–48	Ps. 6
Day 7	Gen. 17–18	Matt. 6:1–18	Ps. 7
Day 8	Gen. 19–20	Matt. 6:19–34	Ps. 8
Day 9	Gen. 21–23	Matt. 7:1–11	Ps. 9:1–8
Day 10	Gen. 24	Matt. 7:12–29	Ps. 9:9–20
Day 11	Gen. 25–26	Matt. 8:1–17	Ps. 10:1–11
Day 12	Gen. 27:1–28:9	Matt. 8:18–34	Ps. 10:12–18
Day 13	Gen. 28:10–29:35	Matt. 9	Ps. 11
Day 14	Gen. 30:1–31:21	Matt. 10:1–15	Ps. 12
Day 15	Gen. 31:22–32:21	Matt. 10:16–36	Ps. 13
Day 16	Gen. 32:22–34:31	Matt. 10:37–11:6	Ps. 14
Day 17	Gen. 35–36	Matt. 11:7–24	Ps. 15
Day 18	Gen. 37–38	Matt. 11:25–30	Ps. 16
Day 19	Gen. 39–40	Matt. 12:1–29	Ps. 17
Day 20	Gen. 41	Matt. 12:30–50	Ps. 18:1–15
Day 21	Gen. 42–43	Matt. 13:1–9	Ps. 18:16–29
Day 22	Gen. 44–45	Matt. 13:10–23	Ps. 18:30–50
Day 23	Gen. 46:1–47:26	Matt. 13:24–43	Ps. 19
Day 24	Gen. 47:27–49:28	Matt. 13:44–58	Ps. 20
Day 25	Gen. 49:29–Exod. 1:22	Matt. 14	Ps. 21
Day 26	Exod. 2–3	Matt. 15:1–28	Ps. 22:1–21
Day 27	Exod. 4:1–5:21	Matt. 15:29–16:12	Ps. 22:22–31
Day 28	Exod. 5:22–7:24	Matt. 16:13–28	Ps. 23
Day 29	Exod. 7:25–9:35	Matt. 17:1–9	Ps. 24
Day 30	Exod. 10–11	Matt. 17:10–27	Ps. 25
Day 31	Exod. 12	Matt. 18:1–20	Ps. 26
Day 32	Exod. 13–14	Matt. 18:21–35	Ps. 27
Day 33	Exod. 15–16	Matt. 19:1–15	Ps. 28
Day 34	Exod. 17–19	Matt. 19:16–30	Ps. 29
Day 35	Exod. 20–21	Matt. 20:1–19	Ps. 30
Day 36	Exod. 22–23	Matt. 20:20–34	Ps. 31:1–8
Day 37	Exod. 24–25	Matt. 21:1–27	Ps. 31:9–18

For inquisitive readers of any age—adults and students alike—here's a book to shed light on the Bible's great questions. Where did the scripture come from? What is God really like? What do some of those confusing Bible passages really mean? More than 400 questions are answered in user-friendly language, based on sound Christian doctrine. Arranged in canonical order, *500 Questions & Answers from the Bible* is an excellent resource for regular Bible study. Its open design presents a wealth of information in an appealing, accessible format—and it's fully illustrated in color!

6" x 9" / 256 pages / Paperback

Available wherever Christian books are sold.